AMERICAN LEGENDS™

"Unsinkable" Molly Brown

Frances E. Ruffin

The Rosen Publishing Group's
PowerKids Press™
New York

For my sister Lola, who has worked hard to keep afloat in this life

Published in 2002 by The Rosen Publishing Group, Inc.
29 East 21st Street, New York, NY 10010

First Edition

Book Design: Michael de Guzman
Project Editor: Kathy Campbell

Photo Credits: pp. 4, 7, 16, 19 © Bettmann/CORBIS; pp. 8, 11, 12 © The Granger Collection, New York; p. 15 © Dave G. Houser/CORBIS; p. 20 (Titanic survivors in lifeboat) © Ralph White/CORBIS and (Titanic survivors board *Carpathia*) © Bettmann/CORBIS.

Ruffin, Frances E.
  "Unsinkable" Molly Brown / Frances E. Ruffin.
      p. cm. — (American legends)
Includes bibliographical references and index.
  ISBN 0-8239-5827-2 (lib. bdg.)
  1. Brown, Margaret Tobin, 1867–1932—Juvenile literature. 2. Titanic (Steamship)—Juvenile literature. 3. Denver (Colo.)—Biography—Juvenile literature. [1. Brown, Margaret Tobin, 1867–1932. 2. Titanic (Steamship) 3. Reformers. 4. Women—Biography.] I. Title. II. American legends (New York, N.Y.)
  CT275.B7656 R84 2002
  978.8'303'092—dc21

                                                                                              00-013090

Manufactured in the United States of America

Contents

The British ship Titanic was said to be the world's fastest and safest ship. It couldn't sink, people claimed. In the early morning of April 15, after it hit an iceberg, the Titanic sank. More than 1,500 people died, partly because there weren't enough lifeboats.

The "Unsinkable" Molly Brown

On the night of April 14, 1912, Mrs. Margaret Brown of Denver, Colorado, enjoyed a dinner with friends aboard the ocean liner the *Titanic*. She was among 2,235 passengers and crew on the *Titanic's* **maiden voyage**, from Southampton, England, to New York, New York. It was the largest and the most **luxurious** passenger ship of its day. It was said the *Titanic* couldn't sink. Mrs. Brown walked along the deck. She glanced at the cold, dark Atlantic Ocean, then entered her room. Hours later, the *Titanic* crashed into an iceberg. The ship sank to the bottom of the sea. Margaret's brave actions to save fellow passengers aboard a lifeboat made her a **heroine** and a **legend**.

What Is a Legend?

A legend is a story that has come down from the past. Sometimes people become legends. Their lives are so interesting that stories are told about them. Parts of the stories, however, might not be true. For example, Margaret Brown led a very eventful life, but "unsinkable" Molly Brown was a made-up name. She was called Maggie, Margaret, or, after her marriage, Mrs. J. J. Brown. Richard Morris, who wrote about her adventure at sea, called her Molly. The name stuck. She has been called Molly ever since in plays and movies about her life. She had never referred to herself as "unsinkable." In fact, a journalist, writing about the *Titanic* experience, referred to her as "the unsinkable Mrs. Brown."

This photograph of Molly Brown was taken in 1927. One legend about Molly claimed that on arriving in New York after the 1912 disaster at sea, she said, "Typical of the Brown luck. I'm unsinkable."

Margaret "Molly" Tobin grew up in Hannibal, Missouri. Hannibal, a port on the Mississippi River, was also the hometown of the writer Samuel Clemens, known as Mark Twain.

Hannibal, Missouri

Molly was born in a modest cottage in Hannibal, Missouri, on July 18, 1867. Her parents named her Margaret Tobin. Her parents, Johanna and John Tobin, were Irish **immigrants**. Both John and Johanna had been **widowed** when they first met in Hannibal. Each already had a young daughter. After their marriage, they had two sons and two more daughters, one of whom was Molly. John Tobin supported his family with the $2.00 each day that he earned as a laborer for the Hannibal Gas Works. As a young girl, Molly was taught school lessons in the home of an aunt. She finished her studies at the age of 13, and worked for a while in a tobacco factory.

Life in Leadville

When her brother Daniel went to seek his fortune in a Colorado mining town, Molly and her sister Helen followed him soon after. In spring 1886, the Tobin sisters arrived in Leadville, Colorado, by train. Molly was 18 years old and anxious to seek her own fortune. Miners from around the world lived in Leadville. It was a silver mining town, but everyone hoped to strike gold. Molly worked in a dry goods store. A few months later, she met the Irishman James Joseph Brown, known to everyone as J. J. He was a mining **engineer**. He was smart and hardworking but not rich. Molly had dreamed of marrying a rich man but instead fell in love with 32-year-old J. J. Brown.

The silver mining town of Leadville had dance halls like this one on State Street for the miners' entertainment. In 1886, Molly and her sister moved to Leadville, which at that time was the second-largest city in Colorado.

Miners gather around a stack of silver bars, called ingots, in Leadville in 1880. Molly's husband, J. J., rose quickly in the mining business. He helped solve a problem with cave-ins at the mine. J. J.'s success helped the Little Jonny Mine find gold.

Molly and J. J.

Molly and J. J. Brown were married in Leadville on September 1, 1886. They moved into J. J.'s two-room cabin on Iron Hill to be closer to the mines. The Browns became busy with their lives as newlyweds. J. J. had worked his way up to become a manager for a large mining company. Molly, wishing to become better educated, studied literature and took voice and piano lessons. She gave birth to their son, Lawrence, in 1887. Their daughter, Catherine, nicknamed Helen, was born two years later. In 1893, Molly and J. J.'s dreams came true. Someone had discovered gold at the Little Jonny Mine, of which J. J. was the manager and part owner. The Browns became rich!

The New Millionaires

In 1894, the Browns moved to a large house, called the House of Lions, in Denver, Colorado. Molly and J. J. began to enjoy a new **lifestyle**. They traveled around the country to visit friends and family. Molly had a hard time being accepted by Denver's rich families. One way she believed she could be accepted was by joining their clubs, so she joined. She also helped to form the Denver Women's Party in 1893, when Colorado became the third state to give women the right to vote in national elections. Molly worked for children's rights, too, by helping to establish a **juvenile** court system. In this system, children who broke the law would not be put in a jail with adult criminals.

With their newfound money, Molly and J. J. bought this mansion, called the House of Lions. It is located on Pennsylvania Street in the wealthy Capitol Hill neighborhood of Denver. Molly soon learned about art and culture and hosted big parties.

Molly Brown is seen here visiting the Hilltop Inn in the wealthy town of Newport, Rhode Island, in 1926. Molly's outspoken nature sometimes upset rich and powerful women, including the socialites of Denver.

A Separation

Molly was happy with her social, **political**, and **public service** activities. One newspaper article described her as having a lively and merry nature. Her nature, the article read, was refreshing but frowned on by Denver's **socialites**. Molly's independence drew attention. Her husband, J. J., grew to resent her activities and the attention she had received as "a favorite personality of Denver's journalists." They decided to end their marriage. In 1909, Molly and J. J. signed a lawful separation agreement. Molly would receive $25,000 of J. J.'s fortune. From this amount, she would be paid $700 every month. She kept ownership of their house and valuable artwork.

A Night of Terror

Molly Brown had become accustomed to traveling around the world alone. Her travels had taken her as far as Egypt and India. Her greatest and saddest travel adventure occurred on the night of April 14, 1912. Molly was reading in her room aboard the *Titanic*. At almost midnight, a strong jolt knocked her out of bed. The ship had hit an iceberg and was sinking. A man banged on her window and ordered her to get her life preserver. Molly only had time to dress in a black velvet suit, her warmest outfit. She pulled on seven pairs of stockings. Then she put on her sable fur coat and a silk cap. Before leaving her room, she tucked $500 into her wallet, strapped on her life belt, and grabbed a 3-inch-high (7.6-cm-high) Egyptian statue for good luck.

When the Titanic *first hit the iceberg, Molly was reading a book in her room. Later investigations about the sinking revealed that warning messages about dangerous icebergs had been received by the ship's crew but had been ignored.*

Right: *Molly and other* Titanic *passengers in* Lifeboat 6 *row toward the rescue ship* Carpathia. *Molly urged everyone to row as hard as they could to try to keep warm.* Left: *The* Carpathia *raises* Lifeboat 6. *Only 705 of the people aboard the* Titanic *lived.*

Into the Icy, Dark Sea

Molly reached the top deck of the *Titanic*, and the air was filled with noise from blasts of steam and rescue rockets. She was surrounded by scared, shouting people, who were pushing to get into lifeboats. The ship had carried only half of the lifeboats necessary to save the number of people aboard. Molly was helped into *Lifeboat 6*. It was large enough to hold 65 people. Only 24 people, including Molly, were aboard when *Lifeboat 6* was lowered into the water. A crew member in the lifeboat insisted that they row away from the *Titanic* as fast as possible. They were in danger of being sucked into the ocean as the ship sank. Molly struggled to keep up the spirits of her boat mates.

Rescue!

Molly and other **survivors** of the disaster watched in terror as the *Titanic* broke apart and disappeared into the Atlantic Ocean. For hours they rowed on a dark, windy sea filled with ice. The *Carpathia* heard the SOS signals from the *Titanic* and came to the rescue. After Molly arrived in New York, she helped to raise money that aided other survivors and their families. She returned to Colorado and ran for the office of U.S. **senator**. She lost the election but spent years onstage as a lecturer on human rights. Molly was living in a hotel in New York when she died of a brain tumor on October 26, 1932. At her death, and even after her death, the "Unsinkable" Molly Brown was the most famous of the *Titanic* survivors.

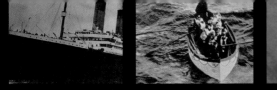

Glossary

engineer (en-jih-NEER) A person who is an expert at planning or building something.

heroine (HER-uh-win) A woman or girl who is brave, does good things, and has a noble character.

immigrants (IH-mih-grints) People who have moved to a new country from another country.

juvenile (JOO-vuh-nyl) Relating to children or young people.

legend (LEH-jend) A story passed down through the years that many people believe.

lifestyle (LYF-styl) The manner in which people live.

luxurious (lug-ZHOOR-ee-us) Something that is beautiful, sometimes expensive, and not really needed.

maiden voyage (MAY-den VOY-ij) A ship's first journey at sea.

political (puh-LIH-tih-kul) Having to do with the work or study of government or public affairs.

public service (PUB-lik SER-vis) Work that is done for the good of all people.

senator (SEH-nuh-ter) A person who is elected to serve in the law-making part of the U.S. government.

socialites (SOH-sheh-lyts) People who are well known in society.

survivors (sur-VY-vurz) People who stay alive despite terrible hardship.

widowed (WIH-dohd) When a person's husband or wife has died.

Index

Web Sites

To learn more about the "Unsinkable" Molly Brown, check out these Web sites:
www.mollybrown.com/intro.html
www.execpc.com/~shepler/mollybrown.html